P9-AOE-094

Earth's Changing Climate
Oceans and Climate Change

WORLD
BOOK

World Book
a Scott Fetzer company
Chicago

Library of Congress Cataloging-in-Publication Data for this volume has been applied for.

Oceans and Climate Change ISBN: 978-0-7166-2710-4

Earth's Changing Climate Set ISBN: 978-0-7166-2705-0

E-book ISBN: 978-0-7166-2720-3 (ePUB3 format)

Printed in China by Toppan Leefung Printing Ltd., Guangdong Province
1st printing October 2015

6546

Staff

Writer: David Dreier

Executive Committee
President
Jim O'Rourke

Vice President and Editor in Chief
Paul A. Kobasa

Vice President, Finance
Donald D. Keller

Director, International Sales
Kristin Norell

Director, Human Resources
Bev Ecker

Editorial

Manager, Annuals/Series Nonfiction
Christine Sullivan

Editor, Annuals/Series Nonfiction
Kendra Muntz

Manager, Science
Jeff De La Rosa

Editors, Science
Will Adams
Echo Gonzalez

Administrative Assistant Annuals/Series Nonfiction
Ethel Matthews

Manager, Contracts & Compliance (Rights & Permissions)
Loranne K. Shields

Manager, Indexing Services
David Pofelski

Manufacturing/ Production

Manufacturing Manager
Sandra Johnson

Production/Technology Manager
Anne Fritzinger

Proofreader
Nathalie Strassheim

Graphics and Design

Senior Art Director
Tom Evans

Senior Designers
Matt Carrington
Isaiah Sheppard
Don Di Sante

Manager, Cartographic Services
Wayne K. Pichler

Senior Cartographer
John M. Rejba

Acknowledgments

Alamy Images: 19 (Steve Morgan), 25 (Jeremy Sutton-Hibbert). AP Images: 43 (Imaginechina). Australian Antarctic Division: 35 (Jonny Stark, Department of the Environment). Getty Images: 17 (Paul Nicklen), 21 (Doug Steakley), 29 (Christopher Pillitz), 41 (Kyle Petrozza, AFP). NASA: 5 (ESA), 13 (Earth Observatory), 39 (Karen L. Nyberg). Science Source: 33 (D.P. Wilson, FLPA). Shutterstock: 7 (Giancarlo Liguori), 9 (Norhayati), 11 (Jamen Percy), 23 (ventdusud), 27 (DAE Photo), 31 (Ethan Daniels), 37 (Willyam Bradberry), 45 (Signature Message). SuperStock: 15 (Mint Images).

Table of contents

Sunrise over the ocean.

© Photo.Lux/Shutterstock

Glossary There is a glossary of terms on page 46. Terms defined in the glossary are in type **that looks like this** on their first appearance on any spread (two facing pages).

Introduction

Earth's oceans are vast and deep. And they are in deep trouble. Human activities are having harmful effects on the oceans of our planet, and many scientists are now worried.

The oceans may seem too big to be affected by human activities. They cover almost two-thirds of Earth's surface and hold nearly all of its water. But their great size does not protect them from our harmful activities.

The oceans are being threatened in several ways. Global warming—also called **climate** change—is the main threat. It is raising ocean temperatures. A related problem is increasing **acid** levels in the oceans. These two events are causing serious problems.

Humans are also harming the oceans by **overfishing.** And by dumping enormous amounts of waste and plastic garbage into the sea.

Although people commonly speak of "the oceans," there is really just one continuous ocean on Earth. It is simply given different names—such as Atlantic and Pacific—for various parts of Earth. In this book, we will call the single worldwide ocean "the oceans." And we will focus on the threats to the oceans that are likely to be caused by climate change.

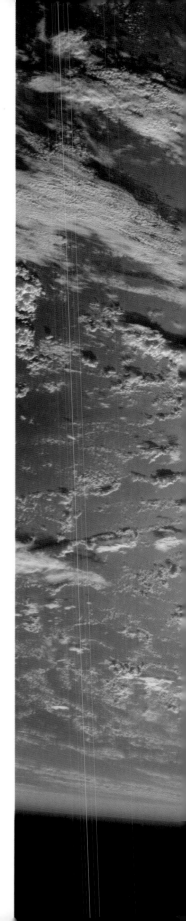

Earth's oceans photographed from space.

Rising temperatures

The oceans are a "heat sink." That means they soak up heat from the **atmosphere** like a sponge soaks up water. The top few feet or meters of ocean water store more heat than all of Earth's atmosphere. That is because water can hold far more heat than can air.

With global warming, Earth's atmosphere has grown steadily warmer. As the atmosphere has warmed, so have the oceans. Since 1900, the temperature of the oceans has increased by an average of 0.13 Fahrenheit degree (0.07 Celsius degree) per decade.

In the early 2000's, the atmosphere continued to warm. However, the rate of warming appeared to be slower. This slowing caused some people to think that global warming was not really happening. But scientists have found that what looked like a slowdown was mostly caused by inaccurate temperature records. Scientists think that once the temperature records are fixed, they will show that the atmosphere has been steadily growing warmer with no slowing at all.

The ocean soaks up heat from the sun.

Global warming vs. climate change

The words *global warming* and *climate change* are often used to mean the same thing. These words are used to mean two very closely linked ideas. Global warming is the recent, *observed* (noticed) increase in **average global surface temperatures** on Earth. Climate change means the changes in **climate** linked to changes in average global temperature. Global average temperature has a complicated effect on climate. Global warming will not cause every place to get warmer. Instead, it will have a variety of effects on temperature, rain and snow, and other parts of climate. These effects are together called *climate change*.

Losing coral reefs

One kind of ocean life affected by global warming is coral. Corals are animals related to jellyfish and sea anemones (uh NEHM uh neez). There are about 2,500 *species* (kinds) of coral. Many species of coral live in large structures called *reefs*. Coral reefs can be found mostly in warm, shallow ocean waters. Many other kinds of ocean life live in and around the reefs. For that reason, coral reefs are sometimes called "the rain forests of the sea."

Reef-building corals live together in large colonies. Each individual coral in the colony is called a *polyp* (POL ihp). The polyps produce a stony material that they use as a skeleton. When a polyp dies, another polyp builds a skeleton on top of the old one. Over many years, the hard material builds up, forming a reef.

Within a coral polyp are living things called **algae.** The algae give the polyps food in return for a place to live. They also give corals their bright colors.

When water temperatures rise, the polyps *expel* (push out) their algae. This condition, which causes the corals to lose their color, is called *bleaching*. Warming ocean waters have caused bleaching in many coral reefs. Unless bleached corals can regain their algae, they eventually die.

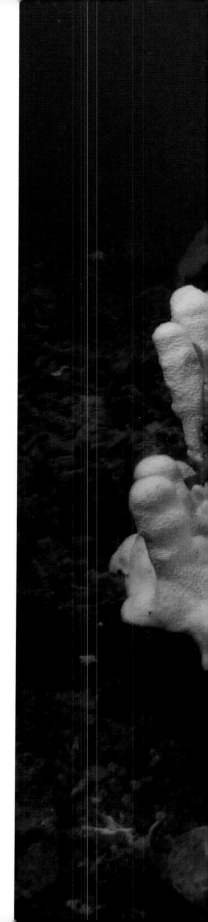

Coral polyps *bleach* (whiten) when they lose the algae that live inside of them.

9

The effect on sea birds

Sea birds are being harmed by **climate** change. These ocean-going birds feed on small fish that swim near the surface. In some areas, these fish are disappearing because of global warming.

There are two main reasons why this happens. First, rising ocean temperatures can cause some fish to move away to cooler ocean waters. Next, warming waters can attract new **predator** fish. The predators eat the smaller fish that had been the food source of seabirds.

One region where the threat to seabirds can be easily seen is the North Atlantic Ocean. Iceland is an island country in this area of the ocean. It is just below the Arctic Circle (see map on page 15). A fish called the *lesser sand eel* is disappearing from the waters around Iceland. Sand eels are the main **prey** of many sea birds. Warmer waters have attracted huge numbers of mackerel fish, which also feed on sand eels. So, the birds have begun hunting and eating a fish called the *snake pipefish*. These fish are much less nutritious than sand eels. And sea-bird chicks have a hard time eating them.

Warmer temperatures caused by climate change are causing sea-bird populations throughout the North Atlantic to shrink, including terns and puffins.

Atlantic puffins in Iceland are threatened by climate change.

11

How warm might the oceans get?

Over the past 100 years, ocean temperatures have risen steadily. The upper levels of the ocean have become about 1.4 Fahrenheit degrees (0.78 Celsius degree) warmer in that time. The average for all ocean water is about 0.32 Fahrenheit degree (0.18 Celsius degree) higher. It takes a tremendous amount of heat to warm the oceans by that much. That heat, scientists say, has come from the **atmosphere.**

Some scientists predict that the **average surface temperature** of the Earth could rise by 3.6 to 10.8 Fahrenheit degrees (2 to 6 Celsius degrees) by the year 2100. Much of this heat added to the atmosphere will be absorbed by the oceans. In this way, the oceans will get increasingly warmer in coming decades.

What if, today, we were to stop all of the activities that are causing this warming of the atmosphere? Scientists say there would still be some continued warming of the oceans. Water temperatures would rise for many years as the oceans slowly *absorbed* (took in) the heat that already exists in the atmosphere.

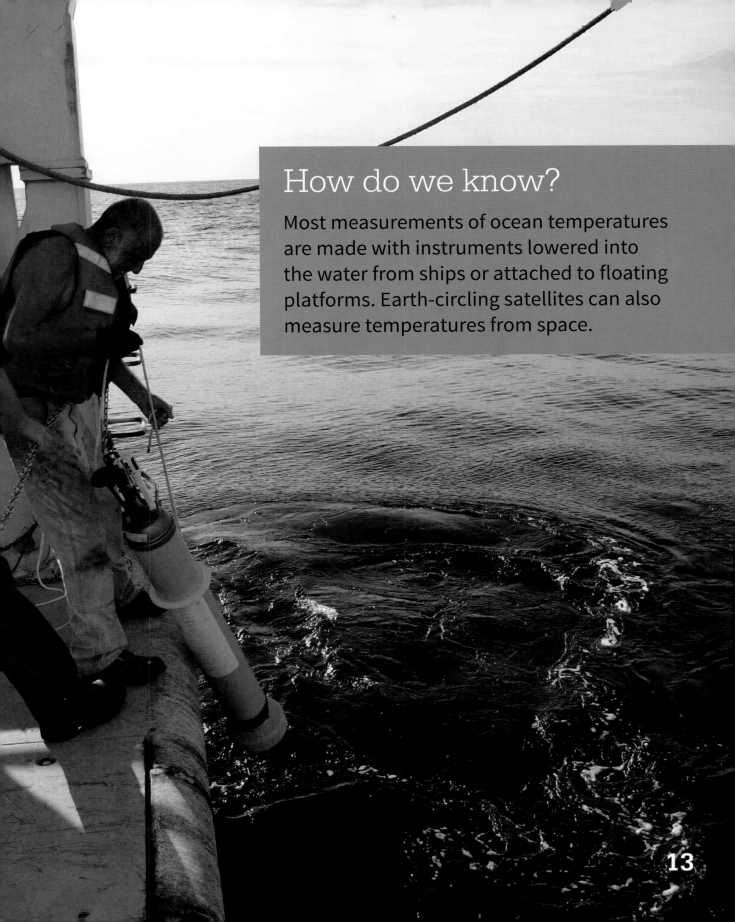

How do we know?

Most measurements of ocean temperatures are made with instruments lowered into the water from ships or attached to floating platforms. Earth-circling satellites can also measure temperatures from space.

Melting ice on land and sea

Much of Earth is covered with ice. Large areas covered in ice reflect sunlight back into space, helping to keep the planet cool. They also serve as *habitats* (places to live) for some *species* (kinds) of animals.

Much of Earth's fresh water is contained in ice on land in the form of *glaciers, ice sheets,* and *icecaps.* A glacier is a slow-moving "river" of ice. An ice sheet is a thick cover of ice and snow on a large area of land. An icecap is a smaller sheet of ice and snow. Another type of ice is *sea ice.* This is seawater that has frozen to form large pieces of floating ice.

Huge areas of ice cover Earth's **polar** regions, the area around the Arctic and Antarctica (see map). The Arctic and Antarctica contain more than 99 percent of Earth's freshwater ice. An ice sheet also covers most of Greenland. The largest island in the world, Greenland is a self-governing territory of Denmark.

With global warming, much ice is melting. The polar ice sheets are getting smaller. And in the Arctic Ocean around the North Pole, large parts of the ocean are now free of ice in the summer.

The loss of sea ice is a threat to animals that depend on it. The next pages will explain why sea ice is so important.

Ice sheets in Antarctica

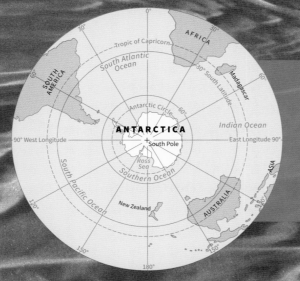

The Arctic is the northernmost region of Earth. It surrounds the North Pole and includes the northern areas of North America, Europe, and Asia.

Antarctica, the land at or near the South Pole, is the coldest and windiest continent on Earth.

Ice and ocean animals

Many seals in Antarctica breed and rest on sea ice, as do penguins. As the ice disappears, the survival of baby seals and penguins is threatened.

Melting sea ice in Arctic waters around the North Pole is harming polar bear populations. The bears hunt for seals from solid platforms of sea ice. With less ice, the bears find it ever harder to obtain food. Some experts fear that polar bears in the wild could become **extinct.**

The loss of sea ice is causing problems below the ice as well as on its surface. Many whales rely on sea ice. One such whale is the *narwhal* (NAHR hwuhl). This small Arctic whale with a long, narrow *tusk* (hornlike growth) spends the winters in ice-covered waters. Warming waters and shifting ice cover are disrupting narwhals' normal movements and feeding. Narwhals are also falling **prey** to killer whales, which have been migrating northward.

In Antarctica, melting sea ice is leading to a loss of tiny shrimplike animals called *krill*. Krill are the main food of blue whales and some penguins and seals. Krill feed on **algae** that grow on the underside of sea ice. But with less ice, there is less algae—and so fewer krill.

A narwhal in Arctic waters

An Arctic "gold rush"

Not everyone views global warming as a disaster in the making. Some people see it as an economic opportunity.

Arctic seas are becoming increasingly ice-free in summer. With open water, it is now possible to **mine** the ocean floor. Beneath the sea floor lie large deposits of oil and natural gas. As much as one-fourth of the world's oil and gas are buried there. Those resources would be worth hundreds of billions of dollars.

No nation owns the North Pole. But countries bordering the Arctic Ocean claim parts of the region. Their **territorial** rights were set in 1982 by the United Nations (UN). This UN agreement gives all ocean-bordering nations ownership of the sea floor for up to 230 miles from their coast.

Five nations around the Arctic have claims on the region: Canada, Denmark, Norway, Russia, and the United States. The nations have agreed that any disagreements over claims to the region will be settled by the UN.

Other sources of wealth in the Arctic Ocean are also possible. The area could become a new fishing area, and many cargo vessels and cruise ships may sail through the ice-free regions. Any of these activities could cause more harm to the Arctic Ocean.

Drilling to explore for oil
in Arctic waters

Sea levels are rising

As glaciers on land, icecaps, and ice sheets melt, the oceans rise. Scientists believe the **sea level** has risen 8 inches (20 centimeters) since 1880. Much of that increase is caused by the melting from ice sheets on Antarctica and Greenland (see map on page 15). When ice floating in the sea melts, it does not raise the sea level. That is because when floating ice melts, it does not change the level of the water it is in.

The melting and freezing of sea ice does have another effect. It changes the *salinity* (saltiness) of the water below it. When seawater freezes, for example, most of the salt gets squeezed out of the ice. That causes the underlying water to get saltier. When ice melts on the other hand, the nearly salt-free water from it mixes with the seawater. This mixing decreases the salinity of the seawater. Such changes are important because the salinity of the water can affect how **currents** flow.

Melting ice is not the only reason for rising sea levels. When water gets warmer, it *expands* (grows) and takes up more *volume* (space). In the decades after 1880, the rise in sea levels resulted mostly from expansion. Since the late 1900's, melting ice from the land has been the main cause.

An ice sheet crashes
into the ocean.

Venice: A vision of the future

Some places in the world are already seeing the effects of rising seas. One of them is the city of Venice in the southern European country of Italy. The people of Venice have long been used to walkways flooded from high **tides.** But the city's flooding problems are likely to get worse in coming years as **sea levels** rise.

Venice is built on 117 islands that lie in **lagoons** on the northeast coast of Italy. Builders constructed the city atop thick wooden **pilings** driven into the soft, wet soil. The city has been slowly settling lower and lower as the pilings sink into the soft ground. Rising sea levels only add to the city's problems.

The leaders of Venice are takings steps to protect their historic city. A system of barriers, or moving walls, are being built that will be used to hold back the Adriatic Sea. The city is also looking at ways to reverse the sinking problem. One leading plan is to force huge amounts of water into the underlying soil. The water would cause the soil to expand and push and hold up the city.

Venice's example is being followed elsewhere as cities located on coasts try to fight future flooding.

Venice in Italy has waterways, called *canals,* in place of many streets. City managers are taking steps to prevent Venice from being covered by rising seawaters.

Disappearing islands

There are places where rising seas are even more of a danger than in Venice. Low-lying islands are especially at risk of being flooded.

The South Pacific nation of Kiribati is already feeling the impact of rising ocean waters. Kiribati is made up of more than 30 tiny **atolls** and islands only a few feet higher than **sea level.** Kiribati could be mostly under water by the year 2050. The nation's 110,000 citizens will be forced to move elsewhere. Kiribati is not alone. Several other island nations, including Maldives, in the Indian Ocean, and Tuvalu, in the South Pacific, are also threatened by rising seas.

It is not only islands that are in danger. Any coastal nation with low-lying lands is at risk. The most endangered coastal nation is probably the South Asian country of Bangladesh. Experts predict that by 2050, about one-fifth of Bangladesh will be flooded. Some 18 million people will have to move to higher ground. And the waters will continue to rise.

Sarichef Island, a part of the state of Alaska in the far north, may become the first U.S. victim of rising seas in America. A village on the island, called Shishmaref, is being *eroded* (worn) away. The coastal village is usually protected from storm waves by sea ice. But the protective ice is disappearing because of global warming. Shishmaref's 600 residents are seeking government help to move away.

Flooding in Kiribati is a problem today. Here, young boys play in floodwaters in Kiribati during an unusually high **tide.** Flooding will become a greater problem for Kiribati as the sea level continues to rise.

How high might the oceans rise?

How much might the oceans rise in coming decades? A group of United Nations experts studied that question. They predicted a rise of 10 to 38 inches (25 to 97 centimeters) by the year 2100. The large gap in those figures is due, in part, to uncertainties about future global warming. If nations greatly reduce the amount of **greenhouse gases** they produce, global warming would slow. The **sea level** rise then would be about 10 inches. On the other hand, continued production of these gases would cause continued ice melting. Greater melting would produce the greatest sea level rise, which could be as high as 38 inches. Even worse, the oceans would continue to rise after that.

The condition of the Antarctic and Greenland ice sheets adds to the uncertainty. Scientists are unsure how rapidly the ice sheets will melt because of **climate** change. Much melting, however, has already occurred.

Some cities are studying ways to deal with rising water. In the United States, New York City officials are looking at constructing a sturdy wall around the island of Manhattan. And Boston, on the Atlantic coast of the United States, is thinking about making itself into an American version of Venice. The Boston plan calls for turning many streets into waterways.

The beach of Gold Coast, a city in Queensland, in the northeast of Australia. Rising sea levels may threaten many cities near the ocean.

What would a world without ice on the land be like?

An Earth without ice on the land would be a much different planet from the one we know today. The world's oceans would be about 220 feet (67 meters) higher. Coastal areas everywhere would be under water. The U.S. state of Florida, the Gulf Coast, and the eastern coast of the United States would be under water.

This disastrous increase in **sea levels** would result mostly from the melting of the Greenland and **Antarctic** ice sheets. Those ice sheets are very large—up to 3 miles (4.7 kilometers) thick in Antarctica. Remember, however, it could take up to 5,000 years for all that ice to melt.

Climate history

Earth's history includes long periods when the planet's lands were without ice and other times when much of the world was frozen.

The last time the lands had no ice, even at the **poles,** was in a warm period called the Eocene (EE uh seen) Epoch (EE pok). It lasted from about 56 million to 34 million years ago. An earlier time of warmth was the Cretaceous Period, from about 145 million to 66 million years ago. This was the Age of Dinosaurs. During this time, sea levels were about 550 feet (168 meters) higher than today.

During the ice ages, ice sheets were spread widely over the land. Sea levels were lower than today because so much water was frozen.

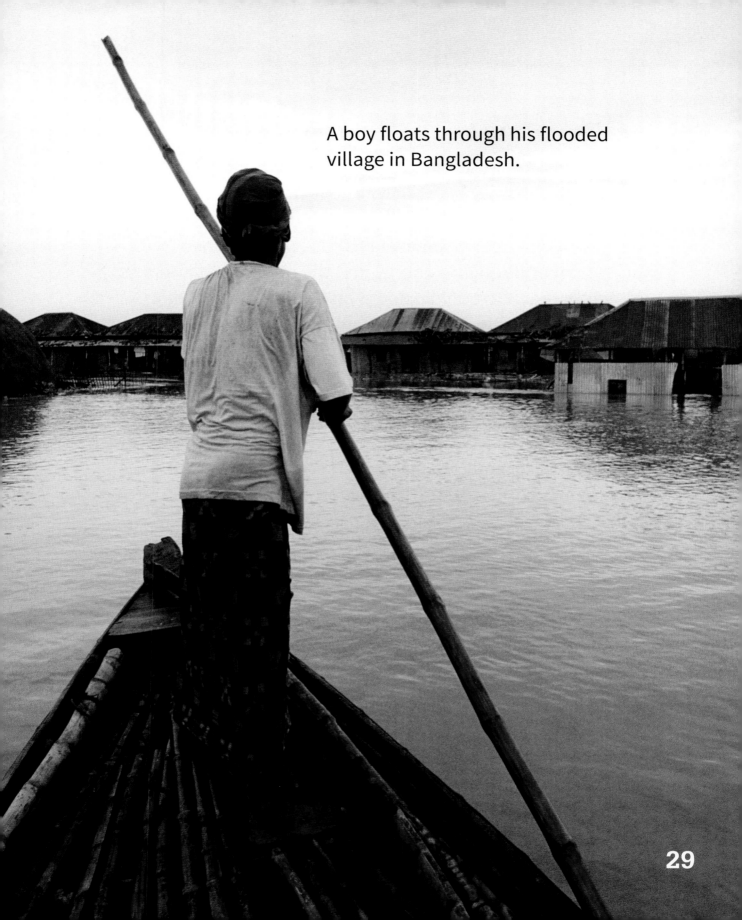

A boy floats through his flooded village in Bangladesh.

The oceans are becoming more acid

The oceans *absorb* (take in) a gas called **carbon dioxide** (CO_2) from the **atmosphere.** Animals produce the gas when their bodies convert food into energy and the material that makes up their bodies. Carbon dioxide is also created by burning anything that contains carbon. Such things include coal, gasoline, and wood.

Green plants use carbon dioxide and the energy of sunlight to grow. In this process they release **oxygen.** This process also occurs in the oceans. Tiny ocean plants called **phytoplankton** (FY toh PLANGK tuhn) use CO_2 in the same way that land plants do. Phytoplankton produce about half of Earth's oxygen.

Much of the CO_2 that gets dissolved in the ocean *reacts* (changes) with seawater. One result of these reactions creates carbon-containing materials called *carbonates*. Many ocean animals, such as corals and oysters, use carbonates and calcium to build their shells.

The chemical reactions in seawater also produce an **acid,** called carbonic acid. For millions of years, this was not a problem. The amount of acid in the oceans remained at a level that was not harmful. That began to change in the 1800's. More CO_2 was released by industry into the atmosphere and absorbed by the oceans. As a result, acid levels in seawater have increased. This could have a bad effect on the shells of many *marine* (ocean) animals.

A coral reef on the coast of the Southeast Asian island nation of Indonesia.

Acidification and ocean life

The increase in levels of **acid** in the oceans is called *acidification* (uh SIHD uh fuh KAY shuhn). The effects of acidification happen deep in the ocean. But many scientists think ocean acidification could be the most serious problem caused by global warming.

Scientists know that acidification limits many ocean animals in building their shells or skeletons. Many marine animals, including oysters, shrimp, and corals, could be affected. One type of Pacific Northwest oyster is already dying out.

Tiny drifting animals called **zooplankton** also build shells. Zooplankton are eaten by small fish, which are in turn eaten by larger fish. Zooplankton cannot survive if they cannot build shells. A big loss of zooplankton from acidification would disrupt the entire ocean **food chain.**

The senses—such as seeing or hearing—of many ocean animals are finely tuned to their watery home. But even small changes in acid levels can damage this. For example, the sense of smell of a fish can be harmed by higher acid levels. Scientists have found that reef-dwelling fish lose their ability to smell **predators.** Predator fish, on the other hand, may lose their ability to smell **prey.** Scientists think that acidification is making it difficult for some fish to reproduce (make more animals like themselves).

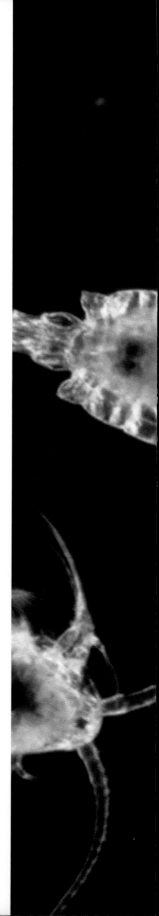

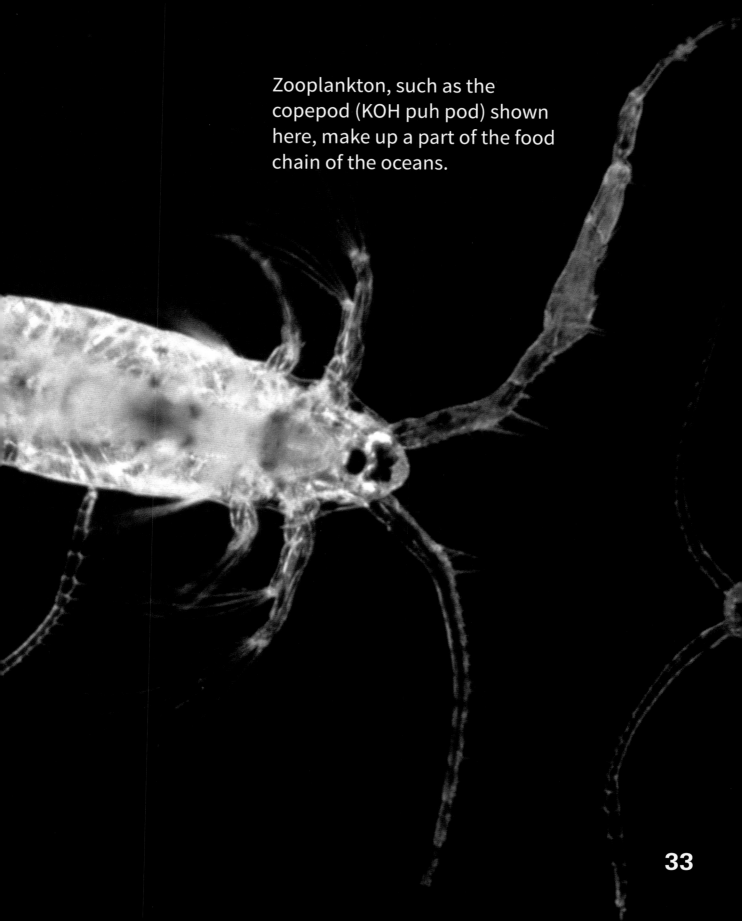

Zooplankton, such as the copepod (KOH puh pod) shown here, make up a part of the food chain of the oceans.

How acid might the oceans get?

Every year, the oceans *absorb* (take in) about 2 billion tons of **carbon dioxide** (CO_2) from the **atmosphere.** Much of that CO_2 is changed into carbonic **acid.** Since the 1800's, the acid level of the oceans has increased by about one-third.

Acidification is now occurring at a very high rate. The rate is many times higher than at any period in history. And it could be the highest that has ever happened. If nations continue to release huge amounts of CO_2, acidification will worsen. By 2050, scientists say, the oceans could be more acidic than they have been for 20 million years.

Measuring acidity

The water of the oceans is not turning into acid. The level of acid is just becoming higher than it was.

The acid level, or acidity, of a liquid is measured with a number called its pH. It is measured on a 14-point scale. Pure water has a pH of 7. Acids have a pH of less than 7. Liquids with a pH greater than 7 are called *alkaline*.

Seawater has a pH of 8.1. It is alkaline. But 200 years ago, water's pH was 8.2. That change may seem small, but it has been enough to harm marine animals. And scientists expect the ocean's acid level to increase.

A scientist conducts an underwater experiment to measure the effect of increasing acid levels on ocean life.

How oceans affect the weather

The oceans affect weather in many ways. The oceans *absorb* (take in) most of the energy from the sun. The most heat is absorbed in regions near Earth's **equator** (the imaginary line that lies between the north and south poles and that circles Earth).

Ocean **currents** are like rivers of moving water within the ocean. Both the **atmosphere** and these currents move heat around the planet from the equator. Much of Earth's weather is affected by these currents.

There are both shallow currents and deep currents. Shallow currents flow in the top 1,000 feet (300 meters) of the oceans. They carry warm water away from the equator. Deep currents flow at lower depths. They carry cold **polar** water toward the equator. It takes water about 1,000 years for it to move through this system of currents.

An event called El Niño (ehl NEEN yoh) happens when a large warm water current arises in tropical waters of the Pacific Ocean. An El Niño happens about every two to seven years, and it can affect the weather throughout the world. In the United States, for example, destructive heavy rains occur in the South and it is drier than normal in the Pacific Northwest during an El Niño year. Since the early 1980's, El Niños have become more frequent and more severe. Scientists think this may be related to global warming.

El Niño has a strong effect on Earth's climate. During an El Niño period, warm water spans the entire Pacific Ocean from Asia to the Americas, instead of centering on Asia. Heavy rains also occur in parts of the Americas during El Niño.

ASIA

Japan

North Pacific Ocean

NORTH AMERICA

North Atlantic Ocean

Tropic of Cancer

Hawaii

Heavy rainfall area

Wind and current

Warm water

Indonesia

Equator 0°

SOUTH AMERICA

Indian Ocean

AUSTRALIA

South Pacific Ocean

New Zealand

Tropic of Capricorn

Map based on data from the National Oceanic and Atmospheric Administration

Typhoon Haiyan

People living near warm seas have long been used to very terrible weather. The warm ocean waters transfer heat and moisture to the **atmosphere,** making huge *rotating* (turning) storms. In the Atlantic and western Pacific Ocean, these storms are called *hurricanes*. In Asia, they are known as *typhoons* or *tropical cyclones.*

Whatever they are called, these storms produce strong winds and heavy rain. They push a mass of water, called a **storm surge,** ahead of them and onto shores.

The people of the Philippines, an island country in the southwest Pacific Ocean, have seen many typhoons. But they had never seen one to match Typhoon Haiyan, which struck in November 2013. Haiyan lashed the island nation with winds of 195 miles (314 kilometers) per hour. It produced a 13-foot (4-meter) storm surge. Haiyan was the most powerful tropical storm in recorded history to reach land. The typhoon killed more than 6,000 people.

What's the connection?

Was it global warming that caused Typhoon Haiyan to be so powerful? Scientists say there is not enough proof to say that it was. Nonetheless, they warn that ever-higher ocean temperatures are likely to make future storms more powerful and destructive.

Preparing for future storms

Storms like Typhoon Haiyan may become common in coming decades. How can nations and communities protect themselves from such terrible storms?

The United Nations (UN) says the first step is education—understanding the dangers of strong storms before they hit. The Philippines is struck by an average of eight or nine typhoons every year. Even so, many Filipinos were unaware of the serious threat posed by a **storm surge.**

Nations and communities are seeking ways to protect areas from very bad weather. Improved construction would help make houses and buildings stronger against high winds and flooding. After Typhoon Haiyan, the Philippines adopted a program to "build back better." New homes will be built stronger.

Barriers, or walls, to stop storm surges could safeguard some regions, such as New Orleans, a city on the Gulf Coast of Louisiana in the south-central United States. But a nation like the Philippines, with low-lying coasts, would be hard to protect. Moving to higher ground might be the only protection against huge storm surges.

A UN conference on **climate** change was held in November 2013. Many nations with a lot of factories admitted that they bear much of the blame for climate change. They promised to help poorer nations cope with stronger storms that may be caused by climate change.

This wall was built to block storm surges in New Orleans, Louisiana.

41

Predicting the future of the oceans

In 2011, a group of ocean scientists issued a frightening report. The researchers said ocean warming and acidification were happening faster.

The researchers also reported on the start of ocean "dead zones." These are regions of the ocean that are low in **oxygen,** a gas that most living things need to survive. Few living things, except **algae,** can survive without oxygen. The low oxygen levels are caused in part by ocean warming—warmer water holds less oxygen.

The report said that the damage being done to the oceans could become impossible to fix. The report made it clear that many kinds of ocean life could die off completely. It urged nations to begin efforts to preserve the oceans before it is too late.

In 2013 and 2014, an organization called the Global Ocean Commission issued its own reports. It too warned of serious threats to the oceans and called for international action.

A photo of an algae-covered beach in Qingdao, China. Oxygen levels in the water in Qingdao are so low that only algae can survive.

What can we do to save the oceans?

Experts agree that the nations of the world must take action together to save the oceans. Reducing nations' production of **carbon dioxide** is an important first step. That action would reduce both the warming and acidification of the seas.

But not all threats to the seas come from climate change. We must also stop dumping plastic and *toxic* (poisonous) waste into the oceans. And nations need to do a better job of preventing the **overfishing** of many kinds of marine life.

There are steps that all of us can take to protect the oceans. Here are a few:

• Eat *sustainable* seafood. "Sustainably caught" means the fish are from populations that are not in danger from overfishing.

• Use less plastic. Plastic pollution in the oceans has reached crisis proportions.

• Support organizations that are working to save the oceans.

• Work to reduce your family's output of carbon dioxide and other **greenhouse gases.** Use special surveys called **carbon footprint** calculators. These help people and organizations to estimate the release of greenhouse gases as a result of their activities and choices. Most things that help conserve energy, like driving less or using less electricity, lower your carbon footprint.

Trash dumped into the ocean washed up on a beach in the Southeast Asian country of Thailand.

GLOSSARY

acid A liquid able, when strong enough, to eat away solids and burn skin.

algae (singular, alga) Simple living things in oceans, lakes, rivers, ponds, and moist soil. Some algae are tiny and are made up of just one cell, but others are large and contain many cells.

atmosphere The mass of gases that surrounds a planet.

atoll A low-lying, ring-shaped island made of coral.

average temperature A temperature for a given time period. For example, in a month, the temperature for each day is totaled, and that number is divided by the number of days in the month, to get the average temperature.

carbon dioxide A colorless gas with no smell found in the atmospheres of many planets, including Earth. On Earth, green plants must get carbon dioxide from the atmosphere to live and grow. Animals breathe out the gas when their bodies convert food into energy. Carbon dioxide is also created by burning things that contain carbon.

carbon footprint A measure of how much greenhouse gas humans add to the atmosphere.

climate The weather of a place averaged over a length of time.

current A flow of water or air.

equator The imaginary line that lies between the north and south poles and that circles Earth. The climate of areas near the equator tends to be warm and rainy.

extinct When every member of a *species* (kind) of living thing has died out.

food chain In a simple example of a food chain, grass is eaten by a rabbit. The rabbit, in turn, is eaten by a fox. The series grass-rabbit-fox forms a food chain.

greenhouse gas Any gas that warms Earth's atmosphere by trapping heat.

mine To dig into the Earth to take out ores, precious metals, coal, oil, or anything valuable.

overfishing Catching fish at a rate faster than they can reproduce.

oxygen A chemical element (O) that is one of the most plentiful elements on Earth. Many living things need oxygen to survive. Animals breathe in the gas, and their bodies use it to convert food into energy. Carbon dioxide is then produced as a waste gas.

phytoplankton Tiny plants, mainly simple one-celled algae, that drift in a body of water. Phytoplankton make up the food for many living things in oceans, lakes, rivers, and ponds.

piling A heavy beam or log driven into the ground to provide support for a building, bridge, or other structure placed upon it.

polar At or near the north or south poles.

predator An animal that eats other animals.

prey Any animal that is hunted or killed for food.

sea level The level of the ocean's surface.

storm surge A rapid rise in sea level that occurs when winds drive ocean waters ashore.

territorial Having to do with a particular region of land.

tides A rise and fall of the ocean level that occurs about every 12 hours each day and that is caused by gravity.

zooplankton Tiny animals that drift in any body of water. Zooplankton are eaten by many larger animals in oceans, lakes, rivers, and ponds.

Books:

Green, Dan, and Simon Basher. *Climate Change.* New York: Kingfisher, 2014.

Kostigen, Thomas. *Extreme Weather: Surviving Tornadoes, Sandstorms, Hailstorms, Blizzards, Hurricanes, and More!* Washington, D.C.: National Geographic, 2014.

Kurlansky, Mark, and Frank Stockton. *World without Fish.* New York: Workman Pub., 2011.

Rothschild, David de. *Earth Matters.* New York: DK Pub., 2011

Websites:

NASA – Oceans of Climate Change
http://climate.nasa.gov/climate_resources/40/

New England Aquarium – Climate Change and the Oceans
http://www.neaq.org/conservation_and_research/climate_change/

United States Environmental Protection Agency – A Student's Guide to Global Climate Change
http://www.epa.gov/climatestudents/

The Nature Conservancy – Carbon footprint calculator
http://www.nature.org/greenliving/carboncalculator/

Think about it:

Try this experiment to see how melting ice in the oceans and on land will affect rising sea levels. Fill a glass with ice cubes, and then fill the glass up almost to the top with water. This glass is a little like the ice in Earth's oceans. On a plate, place several more ice cubes. This plate is a little like ice sheets and glaciers on land. As the ice cubes melt, notice how the water levels change. Does the water run over the edge of either container? Based on what you saw, do you think ice melting in the oceans or on land will cause sea levels to rise? Why?

[Frozen or liquid water take up the same amount of space—scientists would say the *volume* of frozen and liquid water are the same. Because of that, when ice in the oceans melt, sea levels do not rise. When ice on the land melts, that water is added to the water already in the ocean, so sea levels do rise.]

INDEX